THE
10 MINUTE
ART THERAPY GUIDE
ON HOW TO TRANSFORM YOUR LIFE

TAMEKA CONTEÉ

To order additional copies of this book, contact:
Xlibris
844-714-8691
www.Xlibris.com
Orders@Xlibris.com

ISBN: ISBN: 979-8-3694-3152-8 (sc)
         ISBN: 979-8-3694-3153-5 (e)

Library of Congress Control Number: 2024921502

Print information available on the last page

Rev. date: 11/14/2024

For
Chanel-Zoriya,Charles III,
and Charli-Giselle.

Table of Contents

My Journey

Art therapy is most commonly used to treat mental illnesses and can aid in controlling manifestations correlated with psychosocially challenging behaviors, slowing cognitive decline, and enhancing quality of life. Art therapy can help people express themselves more freely, improve their mental health, and enhance interpersonal relationships. The basis of art therapy is established on the idea that people can express themselves more freely, improve their mental health, and enhance interpersonal relationships. It is rooted in the belief that people can recover and feel better through artistic expression.

This is exactly what happened to me. As a teenager, I became severely depressed after having to deal with the unfortunate childhood abandonment issues caused by my father. Like many others who suffer from depression, mine was triggered by a multitude of events, and depression can affect people of all ages. I felt lost, hopeless, and unable to find any solace in my life.

As I transitioned from middle school to high school, I was fortunate that the school I enrolled in had a visual arts program. At that time, art was my favorite subject because it offered me an opportunity to escape my miseries. It wasn't long before my art teacher noticed my skills and wondered why I hadn't taken advantage of the VPA program. She brought this to my mother's attention, and soon after, I auditioned for the program, was accepted, and my schedule was converted, making me a VPA student.

Little did I know, this transition would transform my life and, in many ways, save it. While taking specialized art classes and exploring the program extensively, I slowly began to notice a shift in my desire and zest for life. As I began to create art and express my pent-up emotions through my artistic assignments, my burdens, worries, and stress drastically diminished. Soon, I went on to win art competitions and even national awards for my passionate creations.

In hindsight, as art therapy gained recognition later in my adult life, I realized that I had healed my depression, stress, and anxiety through this very process. This realization amazed me because I vividly remembered times when I didn't care to live, only to later experience moments of euphoria as I became excited about creating art and expressing myself.

In a nutshell, this is the power of art therapy. Though the process may be slow, as it was for me, the positive effects are inevitable. My deep sadness and anguish were transferred into art, depicting broken chains and sweltering fire, like a phoenix rising. These captivating images were viewed as a direct expression of my emotions. This was my healing process—my suppressed emotions suddenly had an outlet, resulting in feeling lighter, free, and excited about life again.

This testimony made me a believer in the art therapy process, and I am certain it can be just as life-saving and healing for you and your loved ones!

How Art Therapy Works

Well, how does it work, you might ask. Let me explain. Art therapy can be a tridirectionally beneficial process, which means that the art a person makes, you, the creator of the art, and the therapist are all working together and offering different components that collectively garner results. Please keep in mind that a person "does not" have to be artistically inclined in order to benefit from art therapy. A person simply has to have an open mind to the possibility of it just working out for them. The art therapy transaction is symbolic communication where images are brought to life from one's unconscious mind.

What art therapy is not is an instructional art class. You will become familiar with art materials and supplies and will be encouraged to play and experiment with those supplies. Expressive art and art therapy primarily have the same benefit. The difference is that art therapy has a precise and structured way to home in and pinpoint specific areas that can be improved in a person's life. It can be very tailored to target and release the necessary emotions that may be bottled up. Expressive Art does not have this level of focus. Furthermore, therapists do not judge, critique, or interpret your artwork unless it is to help one become more aware of what may be taking place on an internal basis. Their job is to assist you with understanding the meaning behind your creation and how it ties into your experiences, and to discuss how to become more self-expressive through art while simultaneously reducing stress and anxiety. To simplify exactly how art therapy works, it is imperative to understand one thing, you are releasing inner feelings in a creative manner, be it musically, literarily, or visually on canvas. Well, you get the picture.

There are many benefits to art therapy. Once you have gone through the steps I just described successfully, the reward is immense. It serves as a healthy outlet for your feelings; it facilitates positive coping skills; and it also reduces pain and anxiety. This factor is helpful for those suffering from an internal illness as well. Art therapy has been known to ease stress and trigger a relaxed state of being. Once a person has mastered the concept of the art therapy process, there are a lot of ways that similar results can be independently obtained, such as through daily journaling. Aside from that, the most optimal way to receive the best results from sessions should be considered anywhere between once a week and once a month.

History Behind Art Therapy

How did art therapy begin? This is a question one might ask as they consider whether to take this approach as a form of therapy for you or someone you may know. Sigmund Freud was one of the first therapists to utilize artist images to help his clients tap into their unconscious thoughts. He also often had his clients draw or illustrate their dreams to express their egos or unconscious desires. This process of artistically expressing oneself has ultimately evolved and transformed over the years. Even with very modernized versions of art therapy techniques and approaches, art therapy would not have come to be without Sigmund Freud's early contributions. Anna Freud, Sigmund Freud's daughter, also used art to communicate with their clients, especially young children. Art therapy is such a comprehensive and unique approach to communicating. It can be understood and beneficial to individuals of all age groups.

One of Sigmund Freud's assistants enjoyed his approach to introducing art to his clients for therapy. He decided to internalize this process and utilize art to act as a guide through his own emotional struggles. With this experimental research and the overwhelming positive outcome relating to improving his own mental health journey, he encouraged others to do the same. The experimental inception of this innovative therapy spurred psychologists, including figures like Margaret Womber and Edith Kramer, to be the trailblazers in formally designating art therapy as its own distinct area of practice. Within their practices, they acknowledged art as a tool used during their therapy sessions with patients. They comprehended and applied the concept of "creating" as a healing aspect, analyzing the art of their patients not for the art itself but for the emotions or thoughts surrounding what motivated the client to paint or draw in a particular manner. Psychologists at this point would work closely with artists to get more insight on how to improve and develop this new age phenomenon called art therapy.

Deciding If Art Therapy Is Right For You

Various forms of art therapy can indeed be very healing for individuals of all ages and mental health needs, based on diverse life experiences. When engaged in art therapy, the process is so effortless that one may barely realize therapy is taking place. In my testimony, I explained how I stumbled across art therapy, only realizing its impact ages later. My passionate and healthy obsession to create and master artistic skills brought me out of depression.

One unique aspect of this therapy is its non-verbal nature. For individuals challenged with expressing feelings verbally, it is easy to release thoughts and achieve similar outcomes through painting or craft making. Trained professionals analyze the created art, interpreting it as though it were a language in itself. If you have faced challenges expressing feelings verbally in traditional counseling, art therapy may be the perfect solution due to its unique design. If you are somewhat creative, this form of therapy is ideal, and you do not have to be a Henri Matisse or Michelangelo to benefit.

Children, in particular, thrive with art therapy, as they are naturally creative and love exploring their wildest imaginations. As we mature into adulthood, we may lose some of those fire-spirited, childlike inhibitions. Nonetheless, art therapy can benefit people of all ages and backgrounds. If you find it challenging to express your feelings in words or seek a non-invasive way to find guidance in your life, art therapy is a type of therapy you should at least try.

10/MINUTE QUICK SURVEY

****

IS ART THERAPY RIGHT FOR YOU OR YOUR CHILD?

Art therapy is ideal for people in all age groups. This unique form of therapy is therapeutic and is suited for persons young and old. Art therapy can help children develop emotionally by expressing their feelings, learn to regulate their emotions and build self-esteem via creative play.

YES or NO: <u>At any point do you or your child struggle with expressing emotions or truly verbalizing your feelings?</u>

Research studies have shown that being in the presence of art can positively impact one's mood and or mental health. Art therapy doesn't depend on the client having artistic capability, no artistic skill is needed to benefit from this form of therapy.

YES or NO: <u>Do you own any art pieces or admire any form of art, such as wall art, poems, music or theatrical content?</u>

Some people believe that starting therapy of any kind including art therapy is a sign of personal failure or incompetence, especially in competitive environments. However, art therapy can be a proactive and exciting step towards personal growth and achieving a well-balanced mental state allowing one to thrive.

YES or NO: <u>Are you in need of a new, inspiring, and fresh way to look at life, or are you in need of finding an easier way to tackle difficult life challenges?</u>

If you selected yes for any of the above questions, then art therapy maybe the perfect solution for you or your child. It may be helpful in many ways such as reducing stress and anxiety, problem solving and improved memory. Reach out to your local art therapist to find more information on starting your mental well-being journey for you or your loved one.

During A Pandemic

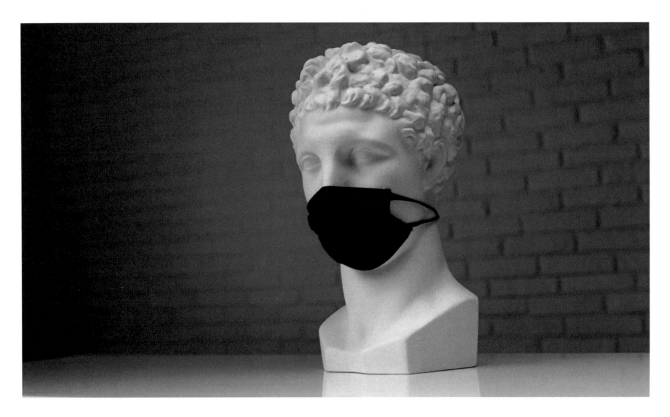

Healthy social development is crucial for thriving in today's society. This is why, collectively, we experience a denial of social interactions during situations such as a pandemic. It becomes imperative to find alternative avenues that balance out areas heavily affected and relate to our mental well-being and stability. Art therapy techniques, among many others, would greatly benefit our society, which strives to discover creative ways to cope with tragic events that can negatively impact many people. During the recent COVID pandemic, which gravely devastated our society on a massive scale, having ways to address the onset of depression could have assisted numerous individuals during this challenging time.

The beauty of art therapy lies in the fact that you do not necessarily need an instructor or therapist present to gain its benefits. Small activities that bring you joy in the comfort of your home are forms of art or creative therapy. What makes this form of therapy unique is that whatever a person chooses as a therapeutic outlet, the goal is to bring a sense of relief and release built-up tension, stress, or emotions. Many do not realize the importance of such practices during a pandemic or otherwise, as they make room for positive and healthy thoughts to develop.

The unfortunate aspect of being in the midst of a lockdown or some form of pandemic is that many outlets individuals normally engage in become unavailable. This further reinforces a negative mindset, escalating to the point where the results can be detrimental. It is crucial to understand that there are other ways and options that can be introduced to assist in these instances. Individuals must first recognize the importance and need for balance, understand that it is attainable during challenging times, and finally, know how to access those resources when challenges present themselves.

Are Paint And Sips Therapeutic?

Paint and Sip parties are a phenomenal event that shook the art and entertainment industry and began to spread like wildfire around 2002. This social activity, which involves painting while sipping a delightful beverage, may also have therapeutic benefits. Let me explain how.

Effective art therapy sessions must always be guided by a certified and trained instructor. This is because a certified therapist provides helpful tips, advice, and guidance on navigating the art-making process to ensure therapeutic benefits for their clients. Paint and Sips, on the other hand, allow plenty of room for self-expression through the painting process, and this is what makes them therapeutic. Participants can freestyle and create art based on their innermost feelings. This is the similarity and the process that ties the two together: the ability to express one's emotions.

If you are looking for a fun way to sit back, socialize, create something cool, release a little stress, or just enjoy a fulfilling pastime, you may be surprised at how a Paint and Sip class can benefit you. However, if you are seeking a very intentional session with the direct goal of achieving positive therapeutic results in your life, then an art therapy session will be much better suited for you.

Addressing the Stigma Of Mental Health

The cultural idea of mental health has shifted over the past few decades. This is perceived as a slow progression, mainly because there is still a long way to go in eradicating the stigma surrounding the topic. Deinstitutionalization has not helped in creating a safe environment for those suffering or in advancing mental health reform. Closing major mental health hospitals around the 1950s was counterproductive in many ways. It heightened the public's perception of what it means to have a mental illness because many patients were released into the community with little to no support, creating a culturally embedded idea that mental health is an uncontrollable issue for those who suffer from it. While this is not necessarily the case, it is how the stigma began. People, in general, must pay attention to their mental health, just like they would see a doctor for a fractured toe or a cold. These issues must be treated, and attention must be paid to these areas, just like mild to moderate mental health issues.

Undeniably, there are many levels and extremes that become factors when discussing mental health. But for the average person, you are not necessarily in the clear. We all, at some point, have a minimum sense of worry about something in our lives, whether it's about our kids' success in a new school or concerns about taking care of an elderly relative. These are mental issues in life that may cause a temporary shift in our mental state, something we all face at some point because we are humans, and mental and physical health are factors in our lives. Art therapy, however, is a sure way to manage one's mental health, and it is easy enough that it can be achieved in the comfort of your own home and practiced in unique ways selected per individual. While we may encounter someone on the street corner severely suffering from a mental health disorder, it's essential to understand that these cases may range from extreme to mild but may simply not be treated. People with mental health issues are no different from those needing medication for physical illnesses.

So the next time you see someone in need on the street corner, take a moment to think deeper about their story and how unfortunate their mental health disorder may be, especially given the current societal setup that doesn't fully consider the rights of people severely suffering from mental health issues. This is a significant concern that requires further attention to shift the perspective and stigma surrounding it. It starts with having more compassion for those suffering from mental health disorders, which can hopefully shift the overall stigma. Once this paradigm has shifted, new progressive pathways, especially through art therapy techniques, can be applied, and greater efforts can be implemented to advance mental health reform and promote healthier lifestyles.

Choosing The Right Therapy For You

Using the creative arts as a form of intervention is designed to be fun, relaxing, and overall enjoyable. These chosen activities, in clever ways, are disguised and can be therapeutic vehicles that guide us toward healing, understanding, balance, and peace within our lives. When someone considers the idea of utilizing any form of art therapy to remedy a current issue or cope with the daily stressors in life, it is crucial for the individual to choose a form of creativity that speaks to one's soul and resonates with them. When it comes to using art therapy in your own private setting without a professional to guide you, it is best to choose an art form that you like. This makes it so much easier to achieve the results one is looking for.

When you are naturally comfortable engaging in a creative outlet, this is a significant key that you may want to move toward when choosing your art therapy activity. For example, if you naturally find yourself drawn to certain types of music that help you relax when you're feeling troubled or stressed, you may want to continue that trend. Writing, painting, crocheting, knitting—any type of creative artistic activity will do when it comes to choosing an activity to get lost in. The idea here is to engage in something that makes you feel good while doing it. This is a significant factor that releases positive signals in your brain that assist with healing and relaxation qualities a person may be looking to achieve. When a person is relaxed, the nervous system is able to effectively quiet itself, causing a balance that translates itself into a therapeutic act benefiting an individual's overall well-being. So, the tip here is to engage in activities you find comfortable and relaxing. There is an entire list to choose from at the end of this book.

Why Art Therapy Should Be A Lifestyle Change

As I begin to detail exactly what art therapy is and how it works, I first want to explain that art therapy has been a lifestyle change for me for quite some time now, and based on the immense benefits, it should be for you too! From a global context, mild to moderate mental health issues are on the rise, primarily due to lack of preventative measures as it relates to health awareness as a whole. The COVID-19 pandemic marked a vast change in the way people interact with each other and has certainly been a factor in the rise of mental health issues for people all over the globe. Just think if your neighbor, coworker, family member or classmate took the time to practice art therapy (which can be done in the comfort of your own home, by the way)—imagine the more balanced and fruitful relationships you could potentially have with those individuals.

You see, when a person's life is in disarray and their mental faculties have been adjusted and are somewhat out of balance, individuals often project that imbalance in their relationships. In everyday terms, it's just like when someone having a bad day takes it out on everyone they come in contact with that day—even the innocent employee making their sandwich for lunch that day. This is by no means the appropriate way to live life. Imagine, however, a world where people had better control over their emotions and how they perceive their circumstances. Through art therapy practices the projection often still takes place, but rather than negativity, it is positive vibes that are delivered and conveyed instead. What a beautiful world that would be! It's a world we all should aspire to, which is why just like you may have an exercise routine and diet you may stick to in order to stay fit and ensure you feel good about yourself, getting into the practice of an art therapy routine is just as important. A lifestyle change is essential to maintaining one's healthy mental state. This also helps to create a healthy and vibrant social environment, which is a vital component of living and thriving in today's society.

So, let us make the moral choice to contribute to the overall quality of being for all in accordance with good standards and mindful conduct towards others. There is far too much violence in schools, heavy drug use amongst our youth, and there are endless reasons why choosing "morality" has become a divisive topic. With these things in mind, there is all the more reason for you and me to commit to positive lifestyle choices.

A New Generation

Bringing significant awareness to the stigma of mental health issues is the single most imperative act needed to eradicate and introduce solutions to the overall issue that so many of our youth are suffering from. We must first identify the issues that start with an individual stance, which spills over to inner family issues, leading to community and society issues. Once the root cause of instability within oneself is recognized, work can begin to transform certain problems we all fall victim to. Our collective world has undeniably faced brand new challenges that we weren't faced with generations ago. Our generation also has staggering advantages that must be taken advantage of and utilized to achieve the abundance that can be created. Mental health is an imperative factor and a key component as our new generation embarks upon this beautiful balancing act. Mental care and healthy mental health practices are gifts that one can give to themselves that nurture the opportunity to thrive in the amazing global landscape.

In the past, this type of self-care has not been highlighted as a highly important factor until now. With this new wave of endless opportunities to connect with one another and share information and data, the time is now for wise words of wisdom and encouragement to begin to set the trend for our new generation. We have a world of information at our fingertips and a universe of knowledge just waiting to be discovered to assist with making this lush world in which we reside a much better place to grow in positive unity. Every decision we make actively shapes and influences our future. I am confident that we are on the right path as long as there are a few concerned individuals who can see and speak to the importance of being in a positive mental health state. We are now even more engaged in creative practices that unknowingly lead us on the path we need to be on regarding this topic.

It's a very exciting time in which we live because we have overcome so many pressing obstacles. That only allows the landscape to tweak and fine-tune the remaining global masterpiece of elevation as our new generation is guided through such an amazing transition. As elders to our new generation, it is our responsibility to also encourage our youth to take pride in the choices that they make. The choices you make, good or bad, begin with your own efforts. As parents, we may give and provide luxury and comfort to our children, which our kids may take pride in. This transaction is definitely a noble one; however, when gifts are glorified and honored more than children taking the time to make good decisions that bring blessings to them, this can be a concern. Valuing the idea of taking responsibility for oneself, knowing how to choose the right path, or having enough mental strength to design and pursue better in life is what our youth should focus on the most. In this day and age, it can be so easy to fall into the trap of "give me, give me, thank you," rather than let me use my mind to take steps to learn to provide for myself, and this mental health practice will take a person much farther. Assist our children by ensuring they are properly armed to make the right decisions, and be proud of them!

PSYCHOLOGY COLOR CHART

RED: Intense, Energetic, Strength, Danger, Associated with food, Nervous, Love, Death, Passion, Anger, Power, Warning, Heat, Hate.

ORANGE: Hot, Aggressive, Success, Unsettled, Joy, Optimism, Playful, Associated with a younger generation or youth, Freedom, Warmth, Creative.

YELLOW: Cheerful, Energetic, Optimistic, Fun, Happy, Intellect, Humor, Rejoice, Bright.

GREEN: Wealth, Nature, Freshness, Easy color for eyes to process, Active, Healthy, Growth, Nourishment, Peace, Love, Jealousy, Guilt.

BLUE: Relaxed, Trust, Security, CORPORATE, Peaceful, Faith, Wisdom, Cool, Controlled, Determination, Goals, Lonely, Tranquil, Masculinity, Coldness, Loyalty, Trust, Intelligence, Subdued, Melancholy.

TEAL: Lovable, Spiritual, Healing, Protection, Sophisticated, Envy, Serenity.

DARK BLUE: Romantic, Calmness and relaxation, Peaceful, Tranquil, Security, Orderly, Good color for marketing.

PINK: Happy, Fun, Respect, Warmth, Health, Sunset, Playful, Femininity, Uncertain.

PURPLE: Royalty, Calming, Mysterious, Imaginative, Meditative, Intuition, Nobility.

WHITE: Clean, Goodness, Innocence, Purity, Fresh, Associated with the medical field, Bored, Easy.

BLACK: Powerful, Formal, Sophisticated, Stressed, Dramatic, Classy, Death, Evil, Mystery, Corruption, Depressed.

BROWN: Friendly, Earth, Outdoors, Longevity, Conservative, Dogmatic, Illness, Soothing.

SILVER: Glamour, High-tech, Sleek, Graceful, Magical, futuristic, associated with releasing emotional mental blocks, Inspires intuition and clairvoyance.

GOLD: Wealth, Prosperity, Valuable, Traditional, Spiritual, Affluence, Success, Champions, Glamour, Wisdom.

THERAPEUTIC ACTIVITIES

Try some of these therapeutic activities to bring in more peace, tranquility, and mental balance, while reducing the stress in your life!

- ✓ Collage making
- ✓ Journaling
- ✓ Listening to music
- ✓ Yoga
- ✓ Mandala drawing
- ✓ Abstract art making
- ✓ Reading a book
- ✓ Clay modeling
- ✓ Meditation
- ✓ Nature drawing
- ✓ Finger painting
- ✓ Dancing
- ✓ Aerobic exercises
- ✓ Playing with a pet
- ✓ Deep breathing
- ✓ Getting a massage
- ✓ Enjoying a hobby

To book an art therapy session with a certified art therapist visit www.conteecreation.com or email artist@conteecreation.com.

Acknowledgment

Many thanks for the universal blessings and support provided to see this project come to pass. A special thanks to Andrew Donaldson for all your hard work and effort in assisting with crafting this literary work of art!

Printed in the United States
by Baker & Taylor Publisher Services